Swimming Grand Canyon and Other Poems

New Women's Voices Series, No. 160

poems by

Rebecca Lawton

Finishing Line Press
Georgetown, Kentucky

Swimming Grand Canyon and Other Poems

New Women's Voices Series, No. 160

Copyright © 2021 by Rebecca Lawton
ISBN 978-1-64662-535-2 First Edition
All rights reserved under International and Pan-American Copyright Conventions. No part of this book may be reproduced in any manner whatsoever without written permission from the publisher, except in the case of brief quotations embodied in critical articles and reviews.

ACKNOWLEDGMENTS

The author is grateful to the following journals, anthologies, and media for publishing or broadcasting these works from *Swimming Grand Canyon and Other Poems*:

"Boatwomen," in *Still Crazy, A Literary Magazine*. Worthington, Ohio. 2011.
"Cougars and Mr. Redford," in *Sonoma Poets Collection II*. Sonoma, California: Hilltop Publishing. 1995.
"Ghost of a River," in *Review*. Salt Lake City, Utah: Utah Wilderness Association. 1993.
"Journal," in *Sonoma Valley Sun*. Sonoma, California: Three House MultiMedia, Inc. 2009.
"Moon River," on *Word by Word*. Rohnert Park, California: KRCB Radio 91.1 fm. 2005.
"On Hearing About Ted," in *The Acorn: A Journal of the Western Sierra*. El Dorado, California: El Dorado Writers' Guild. 1995. (Nominated for Pushcart Prize)
"Seen Near Loma," in *Standing Wave*. Elliot Treichel, editor. Prescott, Arizona. 1997.
"Swimming Grand Canyon" and "The Great Unconformity," in *Going Down Grand: Poems from the Canyon*. Peter Anderson and Rick Kempa, editors. Fruita, Colorado. 2015.

Publisher: Leah Huete de Maines
Editor: Christen Kincaid
Cover Art: Christopher Brown, ChrisBrownPhotography.com
Author Photo: Rebecca Lawton, beccalawton.com
Cover Design: Elizabeth Maines McCleavy

Order online: www.finishinglinepress.com
also available on amazon.com

Author inquiries and mail orders:
Finishing Line Press
PO Box 1626
Georgetown, Kentucky 40324
USA

Contents

Journal 1

First Rapids 2

Swimming Grand Canyon 3

The Cook/Masseuse Encounters Evidence of Global Warming 5

It's Like Life 7

Deubendorff 8

Cinderella 9

Some Say 10

Punta Prieta 11

Moon River 12

On Hearing about Ted 13

Ghost of a River 14

Boatwomen 16

Winter Rivers 17

Delicate Arch 18

The Swiftest Route (for Meriwether Lewis) 19

William Clark 20

The Levee Breach 21

Blake 22

Cougars and Mr. Redford 23

The Great Unconformity (after E.D. McKee) 24

No Debts 25

Other Side of the Rockies 26

Seen Near Loma 27

For Rose, who wanted to swim Hermit

The boat can entrap or liberate. Whether you end up as a boatman or as one liberated depends on your original motive for spiritual work.
—Ram Dass

Journal

At night I'd read its pages
even the names
too beautiful to believe
Matkatamiba
Deer Creek, Thunder River
Elves Chasm, Tapeats Creek
Trout longer than your arm
      in the eddy at Saddle Canyon

Rumpled pages jogged my memory
      about the river
Mudbaths in the Little Colorado
The balmy air at night
when sunbaked wind
      finally cooled enough
          to let us sleep

I remembered the Canyon
Flash floods pouring red
      from Soap Creek, Ryder Canyon
      Nankoweap
During the day, I had to keep moving
The adrenalin at Lava Falls
Crystal, House Rock
The green-blue waters
      of Havasu Creek
and little travertine pools
      to dive in

First Rapids

Your first rapids are small
clever, rumpled sheets
       of silver
They dip and rise
       thrilling when you fall
       and feel

a sudden catch
       in your belly and breath

On stairstep drops
       with headlong plunge
it's a brakeless descent
through boulders
       a trackless trail
       in broken water

No turning back
No way to recall
       the first or last bend

The time to unfall in love
       has passed
There's nothing better
       to die for

Swimming Grand Canyon

I.
Georgie wore leopard print
swimsuits or cyan sunpants
Long ago the wind
leathered her skin

She squinted above my cap
though the sun was not in her eyes
and claimed she didn't mind
flipping boats on the river

A can of beer in both hands
clinging at six in the morning
at Lee's Ferry, she said it again
    Having a boat flip
    in the rapids is a way of life for me
    and an enjoyable one at that

She stood with her lead boatman
smiling, a burly man naked
    from the waist up
Behind them swampers
had been rigging boats
since before dawn

II.
Georgie first swam Grand Canyon
when it was warmer
    before the dam

She started on the river
after the death of her only girl
keeping at it until
she died at eighty-one

She became legend:
Woman of the River

III.
Having a boat flip
means water so cold
it chills your brain
Next your limbs go numb

To fall in water routed
from black-bottomed Lake Powell
is to swim with legs of lead

bound by the rule of fifty
    in fifty-degree water
    it's fifty-fifty
    you'll live fifty minutes

IV.
Georgie always said
if she could find a man
who gave her the same thrill
as the river, she'd marry him

As she spoke she never looked
straight at me
Her stare hurled into the distance
Maybe she saw clearly what was ahead
    and didn't care

Within two years
she'd lost two more:
    one her smiling lead boatman
    one her best friend
    washed out at Lava Falls

Nothing could bring back Rose
    her lost darling

Swimming Grand Canyon
    is a way of life for me
    and an enjoyable one
    at that

The Cook/Masseuse Encounters Evidence of Global Warming

> *"Global, eustatic sea-level rise is about 3.3 meters . . . concentrated along the Pacific and Atlantic seaboards of the United States . . . "*
> —Jonathan L. Bamber et al., "Reassessment of the Potential Sea-Level Rise from a Collapse of the West Antarctic Ice Sheet," *Science*, May 15, 2009

I offered the geologist
the best of my stones
He opened his hands to take them
By day I cooked his meals

By night I kneaded obstinate knots
       from his back

He murmured as he lay face down
*Your claystones drifted west
       off the Cascades*

Call his sense of eons glacial
Call it time learned from the age
of woolly mammoths or dinosaurs

We walked the shore
as our world warmed
He catalogued my stones
and gave me their names
under a sky blue in the way
       a heron's wing is blue

On my table he rolled over
his penis swollen and tidal
like waterlogged lumber
covered with shells
washed up in coastal rivers

His eyes searched for mine
but I looked away
I knew what to do
from long practice—
though I'd never had to
in the heat of summer

When he departed
he kept my best stones
His taxi came at dawn
He left no note

Now the beach has washed away
a mere shard hardly above sea level

Crows pick mussels
Gulls leave toeprints
       on the last spit of sand

Before the geologist left
he told me
Knowledge can save us
       though it hasn't yet
Not even close

It's Like Life

this river story

You start out thinking
it will be simple
there's a right bank
   and a left

all the flow seems to go
    downstream
you think you'll jump on
   and just ride

Then the more you know
the more you see
   it's complicated

You find Lewis and Clark
went *up* the river
They stole land
  and a Clatsop canoe

John Wesley Powell
   had one arm
He did not row himself
but trusted his oarsmen
   until he didn't

Mark Twain came to love
the songs of slaves
   as he loved his words
He chose lightning
not lightning bug
  and a name
   two fathoms deep

Deubendorff

In the Canyon I dodged cameras—
my hair in shreds, face smudged
      with camp grime
clothes mudstained
one step above rags

I'd ditch any lens pointed my way
hide under ballcaps
      —*Disco Sucks* or *King Spud*
      stitched on them for no reason—
buy bits of time
      with one-bird salutes

Now you'll find no pix of me
no white-toothed grins
or arms around boatmen

only the smiles of others
      again and again

Except in one when Lowry
caught me in Deubie
the day I crashed the rock garden
—midair, straight-legged
tossed from the raft
      heels over head—

but no one saw my swim to the beach
      wet crawl from the water
a first-legged fish or star on the run
      desperate to flee
      paparazzi

Cinderella

I didn't think to up and quit
when they called me Cinderella
or gave me the crappiest boat
    in the lineup

I always thought it was just me
    that I should try harder
They were like popular kids
in high school, someone to please

One evening they said
Time you cleaned the port-a-pot
but I had to haul dish pails to camp
so I yelled, *Cinderella!* and she appeared

not in rags but in pink sequined silk
    from her Fairy Godmother
She rode a horse-drawn coach
more like a pumpkin and stepped out
wearing the most crystalline slippers

—clear as the dark sky from
    Nankoweap where starlight
    goes back deep in layers
    like pages in a book by Tolstoy—

She patted her up-do, yawned
and stretched, said in this bored voice
Go fetch my cape, as night had fallen
    and the river's cold settled in

I saw my scheme had failed
even she wouldn't give me my due
    so I finally swore to quit
    when that trip ended

but others said *Don't go*
Your time will come
    and here I still am

Some Say

I.
Dear Wesley, singing his tuneless song
rowed late to camp and the group grew calm
       peaceful and forgiving
Everyone smiled until dark
when he wailed on in his boat
—animal, wounded—

People whispered together
Young girls made faces
We others moved camp away
knowing his pain rose up
       a beast awakened whenever
       his lost squad parted the veil

II.
Some say I knew him well
a stranger when he talked
about trip wires missed by inches
or heads that flew off rotor blades

I turned from him, or he from me
       his hands shaking before the rum
       or heroin kicked in
but I didn't turn from the corpse
       shrunk up in his coffin
—so ancient, coins on his eyes

III.
Some said he'd flown
over mountains, stone peaks
that cast shadow on his
black suit and bones

His child heart stopped
—funny, prescient
       kinder by far than we who live on—
more beautiful by all our river miles
       than his tree-lined grave

Punta Prieta

At Playa La Ballena our eyes shine to see so many sparkling fish, but Juan Chuy says *no es bueno*—it's not what it was only ten years ago when he'd pull *los peces* out in greater numbers in one day than he'll catch now in two weeks—though his face shows no more sorrow than on any morning

He's adapted—*obligado*, so different from *necesito*. His father and grandfather used to fish the whole gulf, paddling one canoe carved from a single trunk cut on the mainland near Mazatlan, where the large trees grow, to build a double-ended boat strutted with thick branches while ours are plastic and glass

Juan and Antonio follow in an open *panga*, their heads bucking as they bounce wave to wave while we paddle up one side and glide down the next to our lunch stop, where Antonio bears a relic up the beach with something like the pride he showed over a platter of sardines he grilled for us yesterday

His gift is a precious piece of wood, dry and light—a shard of canoe Juan handles with tears until Antonio carries it farther to where it won't wash to sea again, then backs away, bowing, as Juan tells me his father stopped paddling when he could no longer catch enough fish to sell and now sits on the seawall at Loreto marina watching one hundred motorized *pangas* bring in thousands of los peces a day and kayaks like ours come and go in pods taking food from the sea

With full bellies we depart Playa La Ballena, leave striped cliffs for the dusky rocks of Punta Prieta, a low-lying point guarding the night's camp, La Playa Bonita, the beautiful beach

When I ask Juan the meaning of *prieta*, he points to the skin on his arms, "Like the tall, dark stranger," though we both know he and Antonio *no es los estraños*—they're only ones here who aren't strangers

Moon River

No river without music
No camp without blues
      part of the scene

Twelve bars anyone could play
      ballads we swore lived
      and died with us

Every trip the same fifty-buck guitar
      six strings and plywood top
slept warm beside me in place of a man

We sang Mancini the way she did
      Ms. Golightly alone on her porch

those Mercer lyrics that were
—and weren't—about a river

She dared them to cut it
over her dead body
      you heartbreaker
      oh dreammaker

They could do that now:
she crossed it in style
      years ago, leaving us

to play the same songs
by the same river
      over and over
      going her way

On Hearing about Ted

Doesn't seem right
though he couldn't stop drinking
and had guns around
He blasted his Airstream
        up through the roof
        mad as hell at the orange cat
We just laughed, shook our heads

In Murphys one winter
drunken and staggering
        hurling sheath knives
        at the new kitchen door
he sneered at our protests
fell dazed to the floor
That guy—we all shrugged—
        is deplorable

But remember his dark eyes
lazy long mustache, shy smile
I saw him first on the road
to Camp Nine and stared, just eighteen
        my friends spoke his name
They said, *Ted looks good on the river*

Remember his straight days
sweet gentle words
When I wrapped on Nameless Rock
disgraced and shivering
I gave up my boat, climbed
out Lumsden Road
Ted took my call and said
        Don't take it hard
        We all make mistakes
        We're here waiting for you, he said

So I thought he'd just shoot
other targets out there
but word's gone around
        He chose himself

Ghost of a River

Witness the dead

Build a wall
for green millions
Eulogize horsetails
that fringed water's edge
        thick, lush as lashes
        tough as old husks

Years ago alder danced
shuddered in hot wind
flamelike and fragrant
        oh sweet decayed catkin

Commemorate summer
and who harbored us
        cottonwood, willow
        live oak, and ash
Inter this gorge
in whisper-thin shroud
Draw haunted cloud down
from dry hills

Color the banks dun
match silted diggers
who lean, frail conspirators
        cones hung in death

Bury this wall
steeped in the stream
that once braided past here
a bright shining ribbon
Set deep this monument
baptized in mother tongue
christened *melones*
        for smooth placer gold

Quarry a headstone
Polish gray marble
that cradled this river
Scour it stone cold
hiss-fine with sand
lustrous as slick slabs
of huge toppled gneiss
        random as tombstones
        in black bottom mud

Then carve for our children
Engrave to remind us
Incise for the living:
        Stanislaus, Stanislaus

Boatwomen

The boatwomen are fifty-three
and fifty-five now
They guided for a living
years ago, their skin like hide
      their hair torn by wind

Both say rowing rapids
      is easier than it was
despite their ruined backs
they can relax
      they don't care
      what people think

Both say the grunt work's harder
than at age twenty and thirty
despite their pinched nerves
      and tendons, ruptured disks
      repaired knees

They know their limits
how to be out of control

The river is the stronger one
      after all
When you're young
you don't get that
      in your gut

Winter Rivers

Now the rivers pour
from wetted throats

They fall down
mud-green slippery
rock-black beds

awaiting seekers
who come in heavy coats
who wander and pray

Now the rivers fill
with dark disks
of earth still falling
still streaming

our mumbled words
and tree roots out to sea

The water has no bones
but carries things we love
with skilled hands

holding steelhead
gray and slick
their damp scales
and morphed jaws

By these waters—
jumbled, chaotic
full of treasure
not worth a dime—

we are far richer
than we thought we'd be

Delicate Arch

I.
Back then you could walk there
alone or with friends you met
up in town or helped down the river

Signs showed the way and
how to take photos to triumph not fail

Pics with no faces or maybe one
smiling, sunshine on sandstone
skies azure as birds

II.
Those desert days past—
a teacher now asks me
> *Why write about dying?*
> *No one will read all*
> *this sadness and death*
>
> *Go try the big new one*
> *where men screw her*
> *over, again and again*
> *It's very well done*

III.
He was smart and admired
I knew he was right
but mentioned the arch
how pictures can fail

but say *it was like*:
> bent rock in synclines
> countless deep grabens
> arches between them
faults cut so close

You can see underneath them
> and sometimes through

The Swiftest Route

—for Meriwether Lewis

You awoke—
the weight of the world fully on you
and dreams gone like geese—
your bones too frail
to bear the thing we call a soul

You rose in darkness
The curve of earth you knew by heart
        fallen away

Birds flew as always before you
—you whose blood thrilled
to the calls of long-eared owls—
who'd felt the pull of western waters

You left at first light, took the swiftest route
near panic, the hour late

When night's cloak lifted, you were still there
        alone among strangers

You who'd named rivers
a second time, who'd claimed
mountains not yours to conquer

Far from your corps, not of your choosing
        not of your plan
away from your men
away from *him*

William Clark

In happier days, by alder trees tapping
on an ocean wind, two men stopped
        one dark and serious

the other red headed, joyful with talk

They'd blazed a route from fort to sea
walked there and back
        as night set in

No one else knew them
by the answering creek
        though I did

Clark spoke of blackberry
        tall Sitka spruce
Lewis cupped palmfuls
        of clear icy water

Clark praised a deer-fern
—and o! the Pacific battering shore—
how much they still could do

Lewis sat quiet, alone in his thoughts
more weary than Christians
done with a quest found empty after all

His eyes caught a stream of elk
endless as it flowed through the woods

I saw them too. I left the men there
        —counting, dreaming
            yearning for what they'd find—
if only they voyaged again

The Levee Breach

The vineyard has flooded again
filled with dark water
through the levee breach

Nothing to do
       til the land dries again
       and creeks settle down
       low in their beds

Blue and green herons
       hunch with old shoulders
woodpeckers cling
to the rough bark of oaks

They don't care no one comes
to the worn rope swing
or old tables grown thick with scrub

in a world full
       of riverbanks, hayfields
          tree roots dangling and homes
undercut on ruined cliffs

We'll patch it all up
against high tides and storms
       men in tall boots
       with muscle and rip-rap

our sinuous levees
—thick earthen snakes—
       racing twinned to the sea

Blake

He visited camp one late fall night

Across the Green River
lay town and the farm
he'd worked all his life
      where plow discs turned up
      stubble and sod
      and magpies lit on earth he'd tumbled

His straw wide-brim hat
      boots low heeled for haying
His tan stopped short at collar and cuffs
as he pulled up my whiskey-crate chair
a thousand deep lines creased his hands

as he drew with a cottonwood stub
      in the dust at his feet

I have ninety-nine acres
of floodplain, he said
and ten on the bench
I keep horses
and I have two sons

So I promised *Then I'll stay on*
when rivers turn to ice
      and summer camps fold
      like bad circus acts

as Blake's sharp eyes, jags of sky blue
shined like two lamps
      clear through me

Cougars and Mr. Redford

Bob you're elusive
like quicksilver lions
who travel by night
       and leave
           big, fresh prints
           in the sand

My friends say
they've seen you
on mountains
       and rivers
He stopped on your day off
and three times before that

Always comes through here
when you look away

Still maybe someday
I'll hear the faint rockfall
       and listen
           for slow pulsing
           footsteps upcanyon

I'll turn, you'll be grinning
—you'll blind me
with brilliance—
then silently wheel
and bound downstream
to freedom

The Great Unconformity

—after E.D. McKee

As much as fifteen thousand feet gone
      the sea broken off
Gaps yawn between strata where
entire islands are lost beneath
      moving sands

When you stop to rest
quartzite cuts your thighs
Sandstone's unforgiving
—though missing millennia
      may surface still—

The break in record if found
would be more than whole lifetimes
      thousands of papers
      yet to write

though you thought
you'd be the one

the man to uncover missing time
      with no sign—maybe
      a hundred million years gone—
and tell its story

No years spent sifting through papers
can be reclaimed, no more than eons
of mountain-building will return

There's only absence
where guidebooks say to look
      beveled schists, stolen history

Your place in
the great unconformity
      clearly preserved downstream
slips out of all memory
the way layers resting
      on upturned rocks, eras erased
stay mute on your life

No Debts

The cobbles sit side by side
They line creekbanks
      and give no thought
to the songs of birds
They make no plans

Some call them mute or dumb
but they gather no moss
and have no debts
or accounts to pay

To be like them
would be wonderful

If I were a stone
especially in the river
I'd wait all my days
for an idea to come
or a friend to call me up

but it might not matter
—I'm like that now—

If Sibley the great
ornithologist passed by
his eyes turned to treetops
and fast flocks of sparrows

of course he would care
if only he'd stop
to dab his sweating face
      and there I'd be
      unable to speak

He would not stoop
to consult me
though I could talk tons
about minerals, earth
      the august patience of stone
and living mortgage free

Other Side of the Rockies

Now I'm back west

of Nanty Glo coal
the big dark Susquehanna
creeks crashing down
through hemlock
mountain laurel

West of black storm-breaking
Indiana, corn in sun and shadow
ponds warm at dawn
near Mulberry Grove

West of oceans of wheat
near Kansas City

All I smell is dust
through rainstorms
through night air

Now I'm back
west of my neighbors
Paul's windchimes and
freezer of pot pies

He'll ride the long switchbacks
past rhododendron and
wild honeysuckle
up Seven Mountains
without me

Seen Near Loma

I.
Forty years ago

Boyce and Sutton drop me at Loma General Store. Sorry, they say, we're driving east to Junction. I shoulder my gear to the edge of Colorado 139, under a yellow cottonwood. They cross the tracks in Boyce's VW over to Interstate 70

Beside me on the ground: guitar, waterproof box, river bag

The first car up the road is a blue Plymouth sedan. It stops, maybe my only chance all day, and I get in. Two ranchers wearing straw Bailey U-Roll-Its drive me past fields of alfalfa and oceans of unfenced grass (green with red purple and yellow wildflowers) over Douglas Pass where aspen and fir grow together and coyotes wail on the ridge

We ride together without speaking, all the way through the Rangely oilfields, pumps bobbing like big-headed pteranodons sucking black oozes

II.
Yesterday

Driving north on 139 past Loma General Store, boarded up long ago. Leaves shudder on the old cottonwood. A figure steps from the shade and moves fast and smooth as a ghost to the edge of the road

On the ground beside him: dusty saddle, saddlebags, old bedroll. A long cigarette dangles from his lips

This time I'm at the wheel. We can drive past fields of alfalfa and colored grasses mixed together like water in a lake, over the pass where coyotes howl, all the way into Rangely

But he's dirty and hard and I don't stop

Rebecca Lawton is an author, fluvial geologist, and former Grand Canyon river guide. She's swum most of the biggest rapids on the Colorado River, often not by choice. She has written about water and human nature in eight books and many journals, including *Aeon, Audubon, Brevity, High Desert Journal, Orion, Sierra, Shenandoah,* and *THEMA*. Her published work in science explores the transport of sediment in rivers, from ephemeral Jurassic streams in northeastern Utah to modern perennial creeks in northern California.

Lawton's honors include a 2020 Nautilus Book Award in Ecology & Environment and 2015 Waterston Desert Writing Prize for *The Oasis This Time: Living and Dying with Water in the West* (Torrey House Press, 2019); 2017 Fulbright Canada RBC Eco Leadership Program Award for work in Victoria, British Columbia; 2014-15 Fulbright Visiting Research Chair at the University of Alberta, Edmonton, to research her second novel *49 North*; 2014 WILLA in original softcover fiction and 2006 Ellen Meloy Award for Desert Writers for her first novel, *Junction, Utah* (Wavegirl, 2013); and three Pushcart Prize nominations in poetry and prose. She's been awarded residencies at Hedgebrook, The Island Institute, Mesa Refuge, and PLAYA.

Her cli-fi collection-in-progress, *Evacuees*, has been excerpted by the Arizona State University Climate Futures Initiative (2018) and in *Chautauqua* (2019). She's also at work on memoir about becoming one of the first Grand Canyon boatwomen.

Lawton holds an M.F.A. in Creative Writing and Literature from Mills College and B.S. with honors in Earth Sciences from the University of California, Santa Cruz. She's a member of the International League of Conservation Writers, International Exchange Alumni, and Authors Guild.

This is her first book of poetry. Read more of her work on her website and blog at beccalawton.com.

www.ingramcontent.com/pod-product-compliance
Lightning Source LLC
LaVergne TN
LVHW041513070426
835507LV00012B/1544